small blessings

Our purpose at Howard Publishing is to:
• *Increase faith* in the hearts of growing Christians
• *Inspire holiness* in the lives of believers
• *Instill hope* in the hearts of struggling people everywhere
        Because He's coming again!

Small Blessings © 2004 by Howard Publishing Co., Inc.
All rights reserved. Printed in China

Small Blessings is produced by becker&mayer! Ltd.
Bellevue, Washington
www.beckermayer.com

Published by Howard Publishing Co., Inc.
3117 North 7th Street, West Monroe, Louisiana 71291-2227

04 05 06 07 08 09 10 11 12 13   10 9 8 7 6 5 4 3 2 1

Edited by Kate Hall and Ben Raker
Designed by Katie LeClercq-Hackworth
Production coordination by Cindy Lashley

ISBN: 1-58229-329-5

small Blessings

illustrations by Erica Becker

HOWARD
PUBLISHING CO.

EVERY DAY IS FILLED WITH LITTLE GIFTS CALLED *small blessings*. These are the simple pleasures that bring joy and meaning to our lives yet often go unnoticed in the hectic pace of day-to-day life. This little book will show you where to start looking for these simple pleasures. Soon you'll be noticing all the small blessings in your life and savoring the enjoyment of each one.

a ladybug
resting on your hand

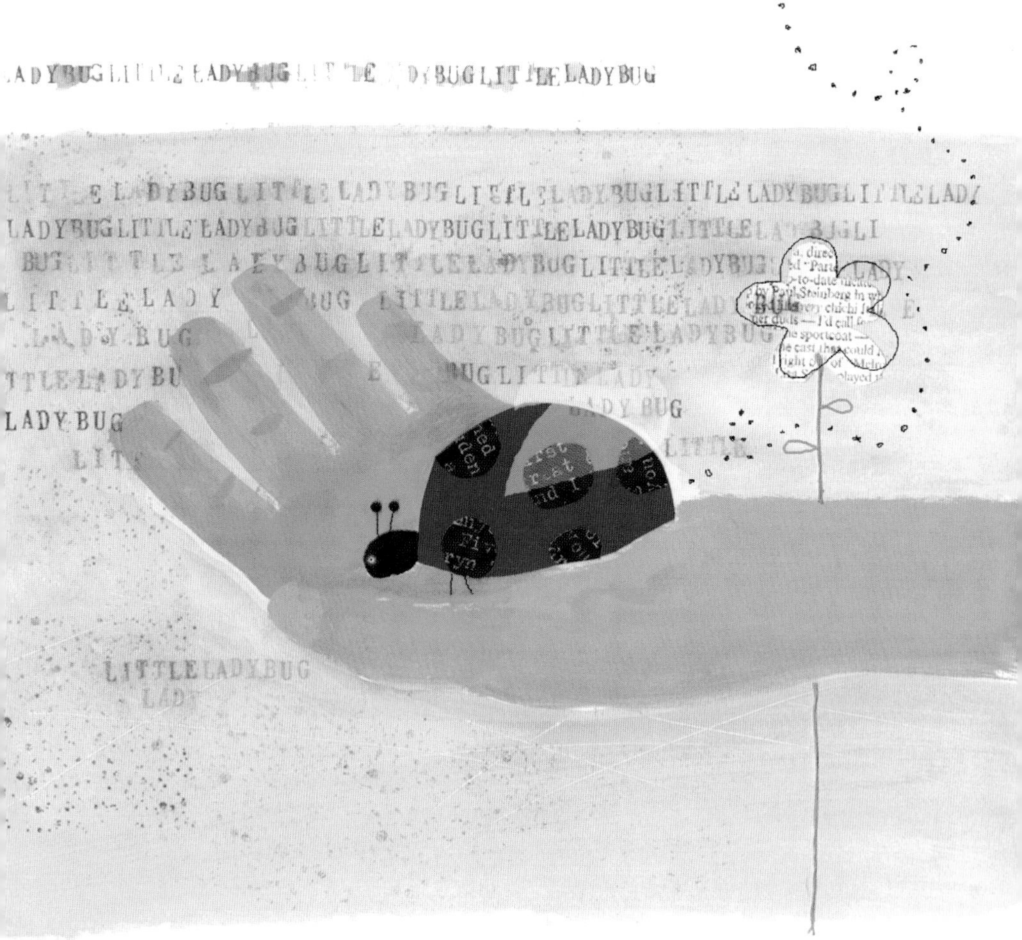
LITTLE LADYBUG

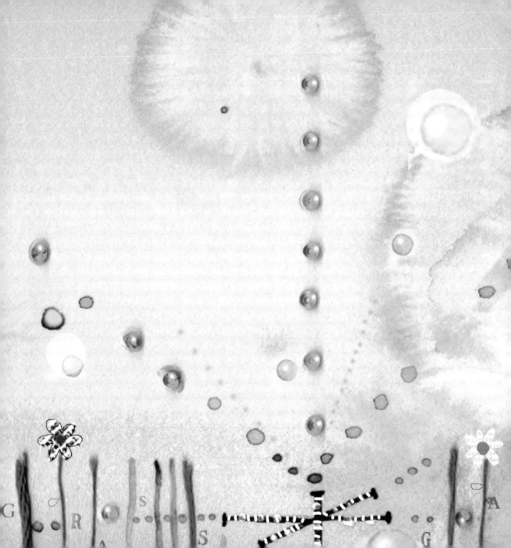

running through a sprinkler

walking past **a bakery shop**
early in the morning

the sun
    warming your face

wildflowers

a reason to celebrate

good friends

WOW!

YOU'RE MY BEST FRIE...
MY BEST FRIEND MY

123456
0378
0594
2763
31500
094253
419

your favorite pajamas

a really good book

a clear, dark night

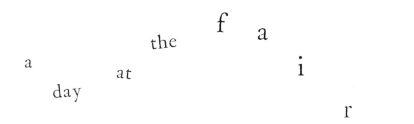

a

the f a

day at i

r

the summer water hole

chocolate

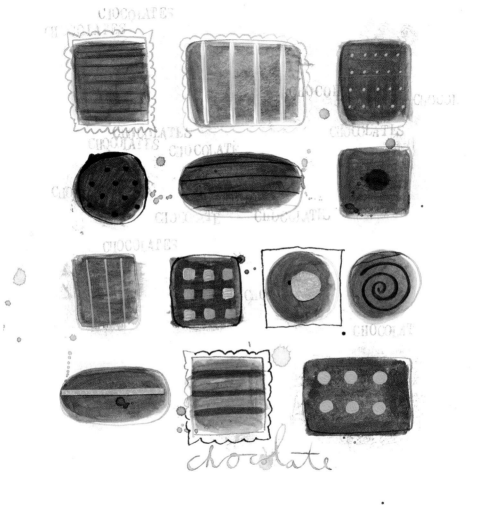

chocolate

picking berries

crocuses
peeping through the snow

window shopping

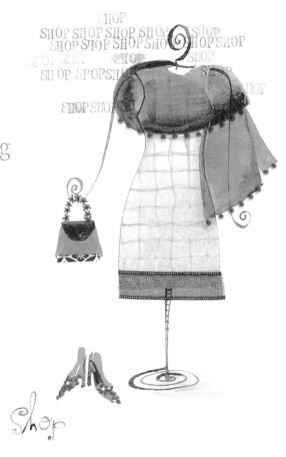

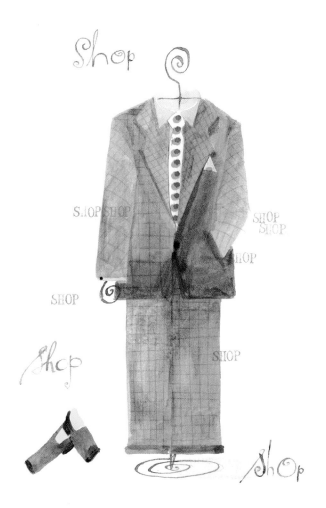

changing
seasons

a cup of steaming coffee
before the rest of the world stirs

bubble baths

making snow angels

a cheerful heart

– from proverbs 17:22

watching **a child** at play

sleeping
with the window open

a crackling fire

bare feet in warm sand

dressing up

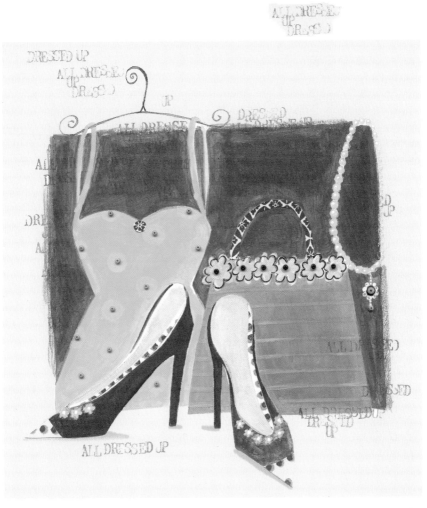

rolling down a grassy hill

singing
     when you think no one is listening

being greeted
by your dog

popcorn and a really good movie

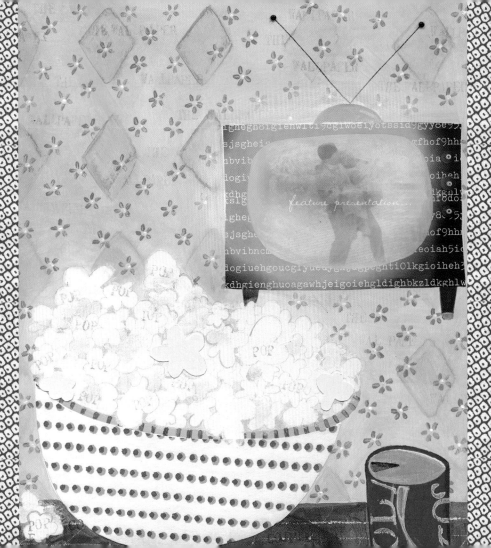

feature presentation...

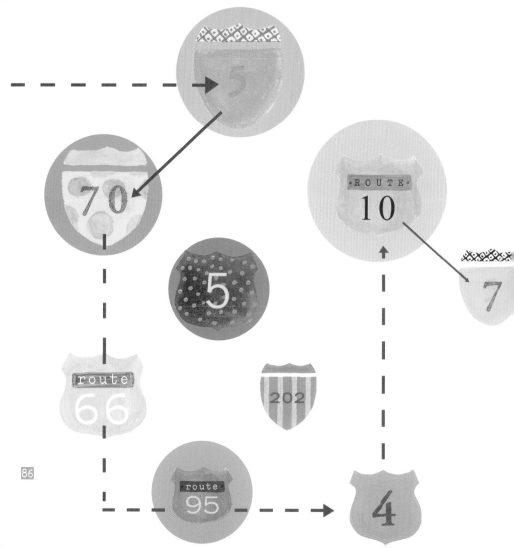

route
80

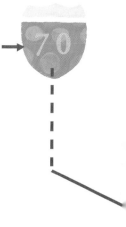

70

475

ROUTE

2

road trips

a summer nap

sharing a treat

walking beside quiet water

– from psalm 23:2b

the end.

IN LOVING MEMORY OF KATIE,
whose friendship and support were
a blessing in my life.

–Erica Becker